STEPH LITTLE

summersdale

OFFICE DARES

Copyright © Summersdale Publishers Ltd, 2005

Reprinted 2005, 2006

Text by Steph Little

Summersdale Publishers Ltd
46 West Street
Chichester
West Sussex
PO19 1RP
UK

www.summersdale.com

Printed and bound in Great Britain

ISBN: 1-84024-453-4
ISBN: 978-1-84024-453-3

About the Author

Steph Little works in a peaceful office in West Sussex and spends her time walking sideways to and from the photocopier. So far, she has never been sacked from a job. She is also the author of *Student Dares*.

Contents

Introduction

The majority of us spend forty hours a week slaving away at a tedious job we do not like, to reach meaningless targets we do not care about, for a soul-sapping boss we have little respect for. But, hurrah — all is not lost. Many of us share the misery of the daily grind but thankfully there is something that can be done.

7

Introduction

Do you feel the urge to spice things up a little? Are you are a non-conformist with a devilish sense of humour?

Now is the time to embrace your inner delinquent. All that is required is this book (small enough to be hidden in any desk drawer), a strong head and an open mind.

Remember we are all in this together and it is up to each and every one of us to make the workplace a little more tolerable.

A quick note about the point system:

The dares have been given a carefully graded point system. Warm yourself up with the 1 point dares: they are perfect for the confident beginner or for your first day with a new company.

The 3 point dares are relatively easy to perform but are often so subtle they may go unnoticed.

10

The 5 point dares are not to be taken lightly. They are challenging and somewhat outrageous. Expect very puzzled glances and to lose friends.

If your contract is coming to an end or if you sense your P45 is looming on the horizon, by all means turn straight to the 10 point dares. Do not blame me for the consequences.

11

WARNING: Playing Office Dares will not reward you with the promotion you have always dreamed of, but rest assured, you will leave the office safe in the knowledge that you have brightened up the day of every employee. Or just confused the hell out of them.

Play the game, if you dare…

At your desk...

While hiding from your boss behind that stack of papers there is a lot of fun to be had using your phone, your work space and your imagination.

1 point dares

Leave a message for a colleague that Mike Rotch/I. P. Freely/Mr T called. Give a fake number, sit back and enjoy listening to them returning the call.

15

Office
DARES

Drink as many cups of coffee as
you can handle. Embrace
the caffeine.

Vacuum around your desk — for half an hour.

17

Drop your chair as low as it will go. Complain loudly that your desk is too high.

Change your company's hold
music to 'Ice Ice Baby'.

Phone someone in the office you barely know, tell them who you are and declare, 'I just called to say I can't talk right now. Bye.'

Keep a fork on your desk so that when your boss asks you to do something, you can look at them through the prongs and imagine them in jail.

Leave a note marked 'URGENT' on a colleague's desk saying, 'I need those figures by lunchtime. This deadline CANNOT be extended.' Leave no contact details.

3 point dares

Ask a colleague to explain something very complicated. Interrupt them mid-way by saying, 'I'm sorry, I don't have time for this. Some of us have got work to do.'

23

Mumble incoherently to a colleague and then say, 'I hope you got that, I don't want to have to repeat myself.'

Create a photo collage of your 'pets' — the more obscure the better, e.g. a blue whale, a condor, a greater bilby.

Bring a framed photograph of
the Royal Family to work and
mount it on the wall. Tell people
it inspires you.

26

Sit on your chair in the lotus position for twenty minutes. If anyone tries to talk to you, look them in the eye and put your finger on your lips.

27

Put mosquito netting around
your work space and play a tape
of tropical sounds all day.

Whenever the office junior
walks by, cough and mutter,
'Minimum wage.'

Bring in a guitar and hold an impromptu sing-a-long on your tea break.

Start each working day by standing on your chair and reading aloud your favourite poem.

5 point dares

Perform yoga at your desk for
an hour at lunchtime
(extra point for wearing Lycra™).

32

Decorate your work space with pictures of the Krankies. Try to pass them off as your children.

Cover the lenses of your glasses
with pictures of eyes cut out of
magazines. Put them on every
time your boss passes your desk.

Wear an unusual sporting uniform to work, e.g. cricket whites, scuba mask, boxing gloves. Tell people you are 'in training'.

Using old cardboard boxes, build a fort around your desk. Tell people they need to ask your permission to enter.

Fashion a long poking device out of office stationery. Use it to stroke your colleague's face while they are on the phone.

To signal the end of a conversation, clamp your hands over your head.

10 point dares

Write an elaborate resignation
letter, detailing your boss's
shortcomings and personal
hygiene problems. Add a P.T.O.
note — 'Only kidding'.

Paint your face to look like a
tiger and roar at your colleagues
whenever they approach you.

Scores

There were a total of 91 points up for grabs in this section.

If you scored 0–20 points: You call yourself daring? You need to raise your game to be in with a chance of being crowned king or queen of the office.

If you scored 21–50 points: A good effort. Now move on to the Meeting Room dares: they will really test your skill.

If you scored 51+ points: Well done! That's the spirit.

In a meeting...

You'll find there are far more daring things to be getting up to than taking notes, nodding your head and pretending to listen.

1 point dares

Demand your colleagues
address you by your wrestling
name, 'Ice Man'.

Instead of taking notes, draw an abstract sketch of your boss. Leave it on the table as you leave.

Spill coffee on the conference
table. Fashion a little paper boat
and sail it down the table.

After every sentence, say 'mon' in a bad Jamaican accent e.g. 'The files are on your desk, mon.'

Bring home-made biscuits. As people start to help themselves, announce that you are struggling with constipation and the main ingredient is a laxative product.

Stand up and demand to know
the real reason the meeting
has been called.

Roll your eyes and shake your head in disagreement each time your superior speaks.

49

Five days in advance of the next meeting, call each of your colleagues to tell them that you are unable to attend as you are not in the mood.

3 point dares

When meeting an associate for the first time, shake hands and insist on a thumb wrestling match.

51

While giving a presentation leave your flies open for one hour. If anyone points it out, reply, 'I know. I really prefer it this way.'

52

Slowly edge your chair
towards the door.

Stare at a female colleague's face. After several minutes say to her, 'I assume it is company policy that women are not allowed to wear make-up.'

54

At the end of a meeting, drop a pen. When someone bends down to pick it up, scream, 'That's mine!' and run away. Later in the day, e-mail them asking them not to touch your belongings in future.

Say to your boss, 'I like your style,' and shoot him with double-barrelled fingers.

56

Kneel in front of the water cooler and drink directly from the water nozzle.

Office DARES

5 point dares

Arrive late, apologise and claim that you didn't have time for lunch so you will be nibbling during the meeting.
Eat an entire raw potato.

58

Bring along a hand puppet, preferably an animal. Ask it to clarify difficult points.

At the end of the meeting, suggest
that, for once, it would be nice
if you concluded with a prayer
(award yourself an extra point if
you launch into it yourself).

Arrange toy figures on the table to represent each meeting attendee. Move them according to the movements of their real-life counterparts.

Present each of your colleagues
with a cup of coffee and a biscuit.
Smash each biscuit with your fist.

Office
DARES

Excuse yourself to go to the
bathroom. Come back with the
entire front of your trousers wet.

63

Cultivate a new accent, e.g. Liverpudlian, Cockney, German.

At a crucial moment, slap your forehead and mutter, 'Shut up, damn it, all of you, just shut up!'

10 point dares

Whilst giving an important presentation replace a simple, frequently used word, such as 'the', with 'bollocks'.

66

When addressing your colleagues, mispronounce their names, e.g. Rob Smith becomes Pob Sniff, Carol Baker becomes Barrel Maker and Sam Bailey becomes Ram Daily.

Scores:

There were a total of 90 points up for grabs in this section.

If you scored 0–20 points: Come on loser, you can do better than that.

If you scored 21–50 points: You're really getting the hang of this now. And you're starting to love it, aren't you?

If you scored 51+ points: Excellent work. Have you noticed your boss's worry lines getting deeper?

At your computer...

How did we all cope before
the days of the Internet and
e-mails? Don't worry, you do
not need to be a technological
wizard to undertake these dares.
All you need is a computer and a
lot of courage.

1 point dares

On arrival at your desk, tell your
computer that you don't want
to fight today and that you are
doing your best.

70

Take your keyboard and sit
under your desk; tap away
energetically.

71

Set the start-up tone of a colleague's PC to a sheep baaing.

Put a chair in front of the printer.
Sit there for an hour and explain
to passers-by that you are waiting
for an important document.

73

Set up a new out of office reply on your PC before your next day off. Some suggestions:

@ Thank you for your message, which has been added to a queuing system. You are currently in 352nd place and you can expect a reply in Julember.

@ I will be out of the office for two weeks for medical reasons. When I return, please refer to me as Bev instead of Dave.

@ I am out of the office today and am therefore unable to delete all the unread, worthless e-mails you send me until my return. Please be patient and your e-mails will be deleted in the order in which they were received.

75

E-mail the whole department
frequently with trivial information
about your whereabouts e.g.
'My office will be closed at
3.42 p.m. for six minutes
while I shred some
important documents.'
Apologise for the inconvenience.

76

3 point dares

Carefully cover your colleague's
PC screen with black paper.
When they have 'problems'
turning it on, tell them that
yours has been giving you
some trouble too
(award yourself an extra point
if they call an IT technician).

77

While you are waiting for documents to print, spin on your chair at high speed and sing 'The Thong Song'.

78

Speed up your boss's mouse so it is uncontrollable. Advise them to cut back on the caffeine.

Send an e-mail to everyone in the company saying that there are cakes for everyone in the kitchen/staff room. When people complain that there were none, lean back, pat your stomach and say, 'Oh, you've got to be faster than that.'

80

Wear rubber gloves whenever you use your PC. If your antics are questioned, simply mutter, 'Infections… everywhere' repeatedly to yourself.

5 point dares

★ ★ ★ ★ ★

Set the screensaver of a colleague's PC to a slideshow of unlikely heart-throbs, e.g. David Hasslehoff, Chesney Hawkes, Pat Sharp...

82

Tamper with the AutoCorrect
feature on a colleague's PC.
Replace their name with 'Chump'.

Change your e-mail address to
the_wolf_man@companyname.com
or
lightning_bolt@companyname.com.

Replace a colleague's mouse with some cheese and a note saying, 'If you don't pay up your mouse gets it.'

Before a colleague arrives, switch keyboards without unplugging them. As they start up their PC, type messages on the screen for them (extra point if they tell you God is talking to them through their computer).

Office DARES

10 point dares

Create a new company letterhead featuring a picture of your favourite superhero. Send out all your boss's correspondence on the new letterhead for a week.

Type up a very detailed e-mail to a 'personal friend' about an STI you have caught. Mention that you find sitting still at your desk very uncomfortable and believe the infection to be highly contagious. Accidentally send the e-mail to everyone in the office.

Scores:

There were a total of 68 points up for grabs in this section.

If you scored 0–25 points: Why are you wasting your time?

If you scored 26–45 points: Great work. Well done.

If you scored 46+ points: You are a shining example of daring behaviour. Bravo!

Office etiquette...

The office is a strange place. Often an eclectic mix of people from all backgrounds and ages can be found in one building. This, to me, sounds like the perfect place for some interesting dares.

Office DARES

1 point dares

Ignore the first five people who
say good morning to you.
Kiss the sixth.

While riding a lift, gasp
dramatically every time
the doors open.

Arrange a staff night out. Make sure your boss is told to arrive 20 minutes before anyone else.

93

Call your colleagues 'Champ' and
'Tiger'. Encourage others to
call you 'Coach'.

Walk sideways to the
photocopier.

Attach a sign that says FAX to
the paper shredder.

No matter what anyone asks you, reply 'OK'. Keep this up for a whole day.

Suggest to your boss that they should hire less attractive cleaners because you find them a distraction.

98

Office
DARES

Announce when you are going to the bathroom. Be sure to specify which number it will be.

Stay behind as everyone else, including the boss, leaves. Thank them for coming.

3 point dares

⭐ ⭐ ⭐

Run a lap of the office at high speed.

Office
DARES

Arrive at work wearing
combats and a balaclava. When
questioned, reply, 'I'm afraid I
can't talk about it.'

Hang a two-foot-long piece of toilet roll from the back of your pants. Act genuinely surprised when someone points it out.

When riding a lift, each time the doors close and it starts its trip to the next floor, hum the *Mission Impossible* theme tune.

Wear an abundance of bling.
Refer to your colleagues as
your 'homeys'.

Office
DARES

Unwrap a Snickers™ bar and
drop it into the toilet. Send
an e-mail to everyone in the
office asking them to be more
considerate when using
the bathroom.

106

Ask the new starter what gender they are. Laugh hysterically at their reply.

Office
DARES

Book a male stripper for the
office on Friday afternoon.

108

Eat a lot of garlic for lunch
for a week. Be sure to breathe
on colleagues.

Make up nicknames for all your colleagues and refer to them only by these names all day. 'No, I'm sorry, I'm going to have to disagree with you there, Chachi.'

110

5 point dares

Arrange for a barbershop quartet to arrive in your boss's office at 9 a.m. Monday morning, singing the national anthem.

On arrival in the morning, kiss everyone in the office on both cheeks. Whisper compliments to the men between kisses, like 'Mmmm, you smell so good.'

When you first encounter your boss in the morning, give him a hug and say, in clear earshot of your colleagues, 'Don't worry, we will get through this together.'

113

Offer to arrange the office
Christmas party. Say you will be
holding it at KFC and charge
everyone £10 each.

If someone offers to make
you a cup of tea, break into
uncontrollable sobs and exclaim,
'That is the nicest thing anyone has
ever said to me.' Ask for a hug.

115

Walk into your boss's office and have this conversation:
'Can you hear that?'
'What?'
'Never mind, it's gone now.'
Repeat at regular intervals throughout the day.

Eat five doughnuts at lunch without licking your lips. If someone points out the sugar on your face, look puzzled and tell them it's your beard (extra point for a female contender).

Office
DARES

Put decaf in the coffeemaker for three weeks. Once everyone has got over their caffeine addictions, switch to espresso.

Walk into a very busy person's office and, while they watch you with growing irritation, turn the light switch off and on ten times.

119

When a colleague of the opposite sex comes to talk to you, hold your hand up to prevent them from speaking and say, 'Look, I know what you're going to ask me... For the last time NO, I will not practise tonsil hockey with you!'

Make yourself a handy office utility belt and fill it with your stationery. Have a stapler in each pocket and wield them like weapons at passing colleagues.

10 point dares

Feign a crush on the oldest and/or least desirable member of staff. Make excuses to be alone with them, insist on pulling out their chair when they sit down, prepare a romantic finger buffet lunch for two… you get the idea.

122

Phone your boss's spouse and tearfully confess to an affair, (give yourself a bonus point if you pretend to be another member of staff).

Scores:

There were a total of 117 points up for grabs in this section.

If you scored 0–40 points: Give this book to someone with balls.

If you scored 41–80 points: Good work. Give yourself a pat on the back.

If you scored 81+ points: Wow. I am in awe of you.

The Grand Total

There were a total of 366 points to be awarded in this book.

If you scored 0–125 points: You're a loser – simple as that. You deserve every moment of office boredom coming to you.

If you scored 126–250 points: Well, you certainly tried didn't you? You deserve a medal for all the stupid things you have done and for all the confusion you have inflicted upon your colleagues.

If you scored 251+ points: You are the ultimate daredevil, on a par with Evil Knievel. You are officially king or queen of the office.

www.summersdale.com